Lightning Bolt Books™

Cross Country Dirt Bike Racing

Rev It Up!

Brianna Kaiser

Lerner Publications ◆ Minneapolis

Lerner Publications Company
An imprint of Lerner Publishing Group, Inc.
241 First Avenue North
Minneapolis, MN 55401 USA

For reading levels and more information, look up this title at www.lernerbooks.com.

Main body text set in Billy Infant Regular. Typeface provided by SparkType.

Editor: Lauren Foley

Library of Congress Cataloging-in-Publication Data

Names: Kaiser, Brianna, 1996- author.
Title: Cross country dirt bike racing : rev it up! / Brianna Kaiser.
Description: Minneapolis : Lerner Publications , [2023] | Series: Lightning Bolt Books — Dirt Bike Zone | Includes bibliographical references and index. | Audience: Ages 6-9 years | Audience: Grades 2-3 | Summary: "Cross country dirt bike racers zoom through woods, deserts, fields, and anywhere else the course takes them. Learn about racing gear, powerful dirt bikes, and the thrilling moments that keep fans coming back for more"— Provided by publisher.
Identifiers: LCCN 2022019856 (print) | LCCN 2022019857 (ebook) | ISBN 9781728476285 (Library Binding) | ISBN 9781728478708 (Paperback) | ISBN 9781728483108 (eBook)
Subjects: LCSH: Motocross—Juvenile literature.
Classification: LCC GV1060.12 .K35 2023 (print) | LCC GV1060.12 (ebook) | DDC 796.7/56—dc23/eng/20220427

LC record available at https://lccn.loc.gov/2022019856
LC ebook record available at https://lccn.loc.gov/2022019857

Manufactured in the United States of America
1-52209-50649-6/21/2022

Table of Contents

One More Lap

After hours of racing on your dirt bike, you're tired. But you keep going. You pass another rider to cross the finish line first. You just won a cross country race!

Cross country is a type of dirt bike race. Dirt bikes are motorcycles that are made for off-road riding only.

All about Cross Country Racing

Cross country races are also called hare scrambles. Riders in the same class race for a set amount of time or number of laps.

Amateur races usually last up to two hours. Pro riders race for up to three hours.

Riders race in classes based on their skills.

Cross country races take place on trails. The trails are several miles long. They can be in woods, deserts, and fields.

A cross country rider races on a sandy trail.

An Enduro rider going up a rocky slope

Cross country racing is similar to Enduro. Enduro is another long dirt bike race. Unlike cross country, Enduro races are done in timed stages.

Riders line up before a race. They have prepared for the long ride.

Cross country riders exercise to prepare for the long race. Exercise helps them have the endurance to finish the race.

There are many cross country series across the US. Different series can have different rules. But many series use the rules set by the American Motorcyclist Association.

Cross country races happen all over the US and around the world.

Ready to Race

Riders can choose from many kinds of dirt bikes. They may prefer certain brands of bikes such as Yamaha and Husqvarna.

Cross country dirt bikes are built to be fast. They are also able to handle the ground, jumps, and turns on the course.

A rider curving around a turn during a cross country race

Riders wear special gear to keep them safe while riding. They wear neck and knee braces, goggles, and a helmet.

A rider puts on his helmet before a race.

They also wear gloves, boots, and a special jacket and pants.

Cross Country Stars and Events

The best riders compete in the AMA West and East Region Hare Scrambles Championship Series and in the Grand National Cross Country (GNCC) Series.

Rachael Archer competed in youth races like this one.

Rachael Archer of New Zealand has been racing since the age of 10. She has competed in the GNCC and won other kinds of dirt bike races.

Ben Kelley got his first dirt bike for his fifth birthday. The rider from Connecticut was the 2021 GNCC champion. He also races in Enduro events.

Dirt bike fans can cheer on these riders, as well as others, in the future.

Bike Diagram

Yamaha WR250F

How It Works

Tire pressure is the amount of air inside a tire. It is measured in pounds per square inch (psi). Riders should check their tire pressure before every race. Most riders use 12 psi. But tire pressure can change depending on the racecourse. Higher tire pressures are good for courses with lots of trees and rocks. Lower tire pressures are good for courses with loose ground like mud or sand.

Glossary

amateur: taking part in an activity without being paid

brand: a kind of dirt bike made by one company

class: a group of riders based on their level

compete: to try to win an event

endurance: the strength and ability needed to last in something such as a cross country race

Enduro: a type of dirt bike racing where riders complete a long race in timed stages

off-road: riding on rough roads, such as dirt or sand

pro: short for professional, taking part in an activity to make money

series: a set of dirt bike races

Learn More

American Motorcyclist Association: Hare Scrambles
https://americanmotorcyclist.com/racing-3/hare-scrambles/

Extreme: MotoX Motocross
https://www.ducksters.com/sports/extrememotox.php

Hogan, Christa C. *Mountain Biking*. Minneapolis: SportsZone, 2020.

Kaiser, Brianna. *Enduro Racing: Rev It Up!* Minneapolis: Lerner Publications, 2023.

Mikoley, Kate. *Off-Road Racing*. New York: Gareth Stevens, 2020.

Motorcycle Racing Facts for Kids
https://kids.kiddle.co/Motorcycle_racing

Index

Photo Acknowledgments

Image credits: Jose Manuel Alvarez Rey/NurPhoto/Getty Images, pp. 4, 14–15; oleksboiko/Shutterstock, p. 5; Pukhov K/Shutterstock, p. 6; Bill Wymar/Alamy Stock Photo, p. 7; Eyal Bartov/Alamy Stock Photo, p. 8; Mustafa Ciftci/Anadolu Agency/Getty Images, p. 9; Nikolay Vinokurov/Alamy Stock Photo, p. 10; Aaron of L.A. Photography/Shutterstock, p. 11; ermess/Shutterstock, p. 12; Ramsey Cardy/Sportsfile/Getty Images, p. 13; Reuters/Lisi Niesner/Alamy Stock Photo, p. 16; Sport/Alamy Stock Photo, p. 17; AP Photo/Markus Berger/Red Bull Content Pool, p. 18; VITAL_ML/Getty Images, p. 19; Aref Barahuie/Shutterstock, p. 20.

Cover: AP Photo/Edoardo Bauer/Red Bull Content Pool.